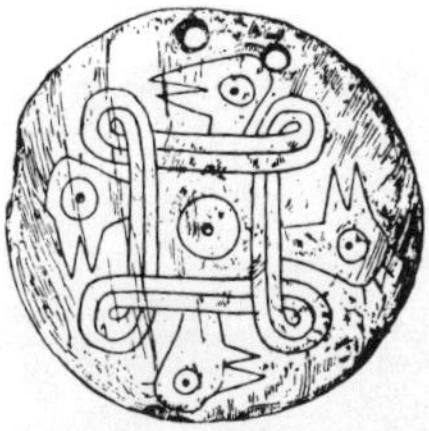

JOHN ROSS

By Sara Gordon Harrell

DILLON PRESS, INC.
MINNEAPOLIS, MINNESOTA

Dillon Press, Inc., 500 South Third Street
Minneapolis, Minnesota 55415

Printed in the United States of America

Library of Congress Cataloging in Publication Data

Harrell, Sara Gordon.
(The Story of an American Indian: 28)

SUMMARY: A biography of the Cherokee chief who led his people for more than 40 years, first in an effort to keep their homeland, and later through their greatest trial when they were forced to go west by the United States government.
1. Ross, John, Cherokee chief, 1790-1866—Juvenile literature. 2. Cherokee Indians — Biography — Juvenile literature. [1. Ross, John, Cherokee chief, 1790-1866. 2. Cherokee Indians — Biography. 3. Indians of North America — Biography] I. Title.
E99.C5R674 970'.004'97 [B] [92] 78-21042

Library of Congress Cataloging in Publication Data

ISBN 0-875-173-2 lib. bdg.

JOHN ROSS

As the principal chief of the Cherokee Nation for forty years, John Ross led his people with courage and honor through the most difficult and tragic time in their history. Born in 1790, he grew up at time when the Cherokees were trying to cope with rapid changes in the world around them. Treaties with the land-hungry Americans ended in broken promises and the loss of Cherokee lands.

In an attempt to withstand the power of the American armies and settlers, the Cherokees adopted many aspects of white culture. They became farmers and ranchers, published their own books and newspaper, and elected their public officials. John Ross led the movement to create a strong central government and constitution for the nation.

Still, the Americans pressed for more and more Cherokee land. In an effort to save the land of his people, John Ross made many trips to Washington and appealed to the Supreme Court of the United States. Finally, seven thousand U.S. troops were sent to the Cherokee homeland to imprison the people in stockades and force them to move west. In 1838 the Cherokees began the tragic one thousand-mile journey to Indian Territory which became known as the Trail of Tears. Nearly one-fourth of the Cherokee Nation died as a result of the Indian removal carried out by the United States government.

Together again in what is now Oklahoma, the Cherokees called once more on John Ross to lead them through a difficult time. Although the nation was divided by the United States Civil War, John Ross continued to serve his people as their leader until his death in 1866.

Contents

CHAPTER I

A Time to Remember

The new moon was rising just beyond the hills, a thin, golden crescent hanging at the top of the mountain. As the sky grew darker, the hills faded. Mists rose from the hollows and curled around the tree trunks, blanketing the earth in silver.

A drum began to beat softly. Soon it was joined by another and another, until the drums sounded like a giant heart beating. Young John Ross looked at his Cherokee friends who sat in a circle around the dying fire. Here, among his people, he felt at home.

It was September and time for the Feast of the Green Corn, an important event in the Cherokee year. By the ancient calendar, it was the month of the seventh moon which was called Maize. The Cherokees no longer used the ancient calendar in the year 1797. Still, they celebrated the Feast of the Green Corn to give thanks for the harvest and to rekindle the sacred fire.

Seven-year-old John Ross, his father, mother, and four brothers and sisters had traveled from their home at Ross's Landing to celebrate the festival with their friends at Hillstown. John's father, Daniel, was not a Cherokee. Born in Scotland, he had come to America to live. There he had met and married John's mother, Mollie McDonald, who was one-quarter Cherokee. After their marriage, Daniel decided to remain in the Cherokee Nation. He didn't take part in the Feast of the Green Corn, but he was accepted as a friend by the Indians and was made welcome.

A sudden silence fell over the crowd. It was time to light the new fire. The flames shot up through the dark night, lighting the faces of the people. Smoke rose into the sky, fragrant with the scent of the seven woods from which the sacred fire was kindled.

On the first day of the ceremony, the men fasted. On the second day, they ate the bitter leaves of herbs to purify themselves. During this time the women prepared the feast which would take place the third day. The children remained away from the square where the ceremony was held, playing in the fields and near the cabins.

John Ross felt at home among his people at the Feast of the Green Corn. This museum display pictures what the feast might have looked like.

Now it was the evening of the third day. Tonight, for the first time, John would be allowed to take part in the feast. The men would drink the "white drink" brewed from the leaves and twigs of a kind of holly. Only the men drank the powerful brew.

The flames crackled and burned higher. Women came and took back coals to their cabins to rekindle the old fires. Finally, the long wait ended, and the feasting began. The good smells of freshly baked bread, ripe corn roasted in the husk, and rich meat stews mixed with the cool night air.

John looked forward to the ghost stories that the elders would tell around the fire. One of his favorites was about a witch called "the Raven Mocker." The Raven Mocker changed magically into a raven, swooping down on dark wings to steal the souls of the dying. Far into the night the Cherokee children listened to the tale tellers' scary stories about the spirits of the animals who lived in their lands.

When the last story had been told, Daniel Ross gathered his sleepy children together for the wagon ride back home. He, too, was pleased with the Feast of the Green Corn. He had asked permission to open a school at Ross's Landing for Cherokee children and had been told yes. He had already spoken to a teacher. Soon his own children and other children would be taught to read and write. They would be taught other things, too, things they would need to know to get along in the fast-changing world of the Cherokees.

At this time the Cherokees were the largest tribe in the Southeast. About twenty thousand Cherokees lived in the forests, mountains, and valleys which made up parts of what is now Georgia, Tennessee, Alabama, Kentucky, and the Carolinas.

We do not know where the word Cherokee comes from. Most likely it was given to them by other tribes. The name they call themselves is *Ani-Yuniwaya,* "the Real, or Principal, People."

A Cherokee legend tells that the people descended from a race of gods who came to the Earth from the sky. According to the legend, the gods traveled to the Earth in flying craft that gathered power from the heavens. And, viewed in the passage of time, it seems that the Cherokees were a bright star indeed.

As far back as ten thousand years ago, campsites were left by a people who hunted and fished and gathered wild berries. Burial mounds appeared about 1000 B.C. The "mound builders" lived in villages built around a flat-topped earthen mound. On top of the mound they kept a sacred fire burning at all times. They farmed and made pottery and jewelry.

In early times the men wore deerskin breechclouts and leather moccasins. The women wore coverings of deerskin and fashioned mantles and shawls from mosses and feathers.

The Spanish explorer, Hernando De Soto, visited the land of the Cherokees in the sixteenth century. He found that the people were living in towns with well-built cabins surrounding a central square. They planted corn, tobacco, squash, and beans on farms in rich valleys where the earth was fertile and moist. Near the farms were streams filled with fish where game animals came to water.

The Cherokees loved the woods and the valleys and the creatures that shared the earth with them. They were an intelligent, questioning people, interested in the world around them. And it was this interest, this search for knowl-

Long ago the Mound Builders built this earthen mound in what would later be the land of the Cherokees.

edge, that Daniel Ross had seen in the Cherokee children.

The family returned to Ross's Landing after the festival. The next day, plans were made to open the school. A teacher was hired and everyone helped to build it.

The schoolhouse was made of logs and had just one large room. At one end the teacher's desk sat near the fireplace. Wooden benches and small desks were made for the students. The desks had tops that lifted up and a place for an inkwell. Grooves carved in the top held the lead plummets that the children used for writing in their notebooks.

Since the Cherokees did not yet have a written language, the students were taught to read and write English. The young Cherokees read and listened to the same stories that children everywhere loved. John discovered the island of *Robinson Crusoe* and the magical land in *Gulliver's Travels*.

Soon other schools were started for the Cherokee children. Moravian missionaries established a school called Spring Place in Georgia. Presbyterians and Baptists opened mission schools, and many missionaries made their homes in the nation. At first, the missionaries were told that no religion should be taught. But as time passed, more and more Cherokees became Christians.

When John first entered school, he was called "Little John" by his friends. He was small for his age, but he made up for his size by running faster, studying longer, and trying harder than anyone else in his class. The other children looked on John as a leader. He was proud to be a Cherokee.

CHAPTER II

Ross's Landing

From the mountaintop and as far as he could see, there were miles and miles of thick forests. Down below, the Tennessee River rolled across the land like a blue silk ribbon unfurled by a giant hand. Sourwood trees blazed scarlet against the deep green of the woods. Soon the other trees would change their colors, and the hills would blaze in the glory of autumn.

By the distant river John could see his home and the ferry and the trading post. Ross's Landing was a busy place. People came from miles away to cross the river on the ferry. When he was not in school, John helped his father at the ferry and at the trading post which he owned.

The trading post was filled with supplies and goods used by both the Indians and the whites who traveled through the nation. On a large table furs and deerskins were piled in great heaps. Bolts of calico cloth and linen were stacked on the shelves against the wall. Glass jars filled with peppermint drops and rock candy stood on the counter top. There were soft deerskin moccasins, skillfully beaded and sewn by the Cherokee women. Wampum belts, embroidered in designs of beads and porcupine quills, told the history of the Cherokees. These belts were prized by both whites and Indians.

From the mountaintop John could look out over many miles of the beautiful Cherokee homeland.

The Ross home was not far from the trading post. It sat on a gentle rise overlooking the river. Maple trees shaded the wide porches, and a split-rail fence surrounded the house. The front garden bloomed with bright flowers planted by John's mother. Near the house were an apple orchard and pear trees.

From the mountain John looked for his pony in the meadow next to the house. Riding with his friends, he had explored the valleys and forests of the rolling, fertile lands. He and his brothers and sisters had dug the tender roots of sassafras with which his mother brewed a fragrant pink tea. They had fished the streams for the tiny sweet bream that his mother dipped in batter and fried.

John knew where the plumpest wild plums grew and where to find the best chinquapins. He knew when the scuppermongs were ripe and where to find the tiny fox grapes that grew wild in the woods.

A group of children ran from the house and out into the meadow. John watched to see if they were checking the beehives dotted along the edge of the fence. His father kept bees, and the hives were busy now. The bees were making honey from the scarlet sourwood trees that dotted the hills.

There were nine young Rosses, counting the new baby who had just been born. John and his brother Lewis were leaving Ross's Landing to attend private school in Kingston, Tennessee. They would stay with family friends, the Clarks, in Kingston. John's father had arranged for the boys to help Thomas Clark in his business to help earn their keep.

John did not want to leave the small school and his home at Ross's Landing. He had good friends there. One friend was John Ridge, whose father was a powerful man in the nation. He was called simply, "The Ridge." They had a home not far from the Ross home.

John was a good student and had learned the story of the Cherokee Nation very well. At the time he entered school, there was no Cherokee alphabet. History was taught through stories told to children by parents and tribal elders.

John knew the story of Chief Attacullaculla, who was the leader of the first Cherokee group to visit England. While there, the Cherokees signed a treaty in which they agreed to trade only with the British. They also agreed to fight for England should they be called upon in time of war.

As time went by, both French and British traders began working the trade routes into the Cherokee Nation. The whites brought diseases for which the native Americans had no defense. In 1738 an outbreak of smallpox destroyed nearly half the Cherokee people. Those who survived were horribly scarred. Many took their own lives after seeing their scarred faces and bodies mirrored in the streams.

Although weakened in strength and number by the pox, the Cherokees were called upon to honor their treaty with the British by fighting for them in the French and Indian War. An officer in that war was Colonel George Washington, who was a friend to the Cherokees. He urged his men to respect the Indian people. Most of them did, but later a few colonists massacred twenty-four Indians. When the Cherokees struck back, a local war broke out. The settlers attacked the Cherokee homeland, destroying farms, animals, and crops.

Because the Cherokees fought on the side of the British during the American Revolution, the Cherokee people suffered greatly once more. The nation was attacked by American troops from Virginia, the Carolinas, and Georgia. When the war ended, a second outbreak of smallpox threatened to destroy the little that remained of the nation.

Cherokee leaders were called to Hopewell, South Carolina, to sign a peace treaty with the Americans. For the first time the Cherokees were treated as a nation. There were no demands by the Americans for Cherokee land. The treaty declared that the Cherokees were under the protection of

The first group of Cherokee leaders to visit England signed a treaty of trade and friendship with the British.

the United States. It also said that the two nations would be friends from that day.

But even as the treaty was being signed, land-hungry settlers were moving onto Cherokee lands to claim them for their own use. The Indians protested to the Congress of the United States. In response, Secretary of State Henry Knox wrote the first Indian policy for the United States. But he protested to President Washington that the policies were not good unless they could be backed up strongly by the federal government. He was upset at the treatment of the Indians and the takeover of Indian lands by white Americans.

The Holston Treaty was signed into law the year after John was born. Soon afterward, his father moved the family to the place on the Tennessee River known as Ross's Landing. When John and Lewis left to go to school at Kingston, Daniel Ross wished them well and told them to study hard. John was a bright student who learned his lessons well. He also learned much about the white way of life that would serve him well in later years.

Three years later, when John was eighteen, he was called home due to the death of his mother. This was the end of his formal education.

John had grown up with stories of treaties and broken promises. Now that he was a young man, he set to work to serve the nation. John was a Cherokee, and he had high hopes for his people.

CHAPTER III

A New Leader, a New Way

John Ross rode through the streets of Ustanali on his way to the council meeting. Ustanali had been chosen as the new capital of the Cherokee Nation, taking the place of Echota, the ancient capital. As more and more white settlers moved onto Indian lands, the white settlements had grown too close to Echota.

John was excited. For the first time he was to speak before the entire council. He wanted to do well, but he was prepared for a fight. Though he knew that some of the men on the council would resent it, he intended to give his speech in English. One man in particular would not be pleased—a man respected by John and by all of the Cherokees who was called "The Ridge."

He was so named because of his wisdom and his ability to see through problems and work them out. The Cherokees felt that he was like a man standing on a ridge, looking out over the lands, able to see farther than most people. At the time of the council meeting, he was one of the most powerful men in the nation.

The meeting was called to order, and John Ross was introduced. When John began his speech in English, The Ridge protested. "Speak the Cherokee language," he said.

At the time John spoke before the council, The Ridge was a powerful and respected Cherokee leader. (Courtesy Oklahoma Historical Society)

But he was overruled by the other members of the council, who allowed John to finish speaking.

John spoke of the many changes taking place within the Cherokee Nation. Until 1800, western Georgia had been Indian land. But as Georgia's white population grew, settlers came to the Indian lands and claimed them as their own.

John urged the Cherokees to join together to create a strong central government. In the past, unity had not been the Indian way. People shared the land, and each tribe protected its own hunting grounds. The land was held as a trust. This was one of the reasons the whites had been able to take the land so easily. John wanted this changed.

What was needed, he said, was a strong, unified Indian nation. That was the best way to fight the takeover of lands by whites. Since the whites were powerful, the Indians had to become powerful, too. Already, he reminded them, Cherokees had begun to move west into Arkansas, on the border of what was known as Indian Territory. Any moves out of the eastern homeland weakened the nation.

When John finished his speech, the council was much impressed. So was the new U.S. Indian agent, Colonel Return J. Meigs. He chose John to visit the Cherokee settlements in the West and to bring back word on how they were faring.

At the end of the meeting, John left for the West. On his trip he met a young Tennessee frontiersman named Andrew Jackson. Their paths would cross many times.

For the next few years, the nation made great progress in strengthening its government. Schools were opened and new roads built. More and more Cherokees began farming large tracts of land and building fine houses. While men like John Ross and The Ridge were happy with the progress, other Indians were not at all happy with the Cherokees' acceptance of white culture. One such man was the great Shawnee leader, Tecumseh.

Tecumseh traveled from tribe to tribe, urging the people to unite in a strong force to save Indian land from the white settlers. He asked his brothers and sisters to return to the ancient ways, to give up the "white man's clothes and trinkets." He told them to "throw away their mills and looms, kill their cats, put on paint and buckskin and be Indians once again."

Many of the Creek Indians who listened to Tecumseh liked what he had to say. The Creeks were threatened with the loss of their lands, and they needed a strong leader. Many thought that Tecumseh was the leader they so desperately needed. Some of them sent word to the Cherokees. "Listen," they said, "and take heed."

When Tecumseh came to the land of the Cherokees, John Ross, The Ridge, and forty-eight other chiefs traveled to hear him. "Once our people were many," said Tecumseh. "Once we owned the land from the sunrise to the sunset. Once our campfires twinkled at night like the stars of a fallen sky. Then the white man came. Our campfires dwindled.

"Everywhere our people have passed away, as the snow of the mountains melts in May. We no longer rule the forest. The game has gone like our hunting grounds. Even our lands are nearly gone. Yes, my brothers, our campfires are few. Those that still burn we must draw together.

"Behold what the white man has done to our people! Gone are the Pequot, the Narraganset, the Powhatan, the Tuscarora, and the Coree. . . . Soon there will be no place for the Cherokee to hunt the deer and the bear. The tomahawk of the Shawnee is ready. Will the Cherokee raise the tomahawk? Will the Cherokee join their brothers the Shawnee?"

After his speech a medicine dance was held at Ustanali where Tecumseh's plans were told to the people. But his words went against what the Cherokees saw as their future. Their goals were what John Ross had called for—unity through education and progress. "We have turned away our ears," said The Ridge. And John Ross agreed. Tecumseh's message would not be good for the Cherokee people.

Many American Indians did listen to Tecumseh and pledged their support to his cause. In 1812, when the United States declared war on Great Britain, Tecumseh gathered a force of two thousand warriors to fight for the British. Soon the news of the war spread throughout the Cherokee Nation.

For almost thirty years the Cherokees had maintained a "no war" policy. Through the influence of John Ross, The Ridge, and other leaders, the Cherokees did not join Tecumseh's warriors against the forces of the United States. The Cherokees remembered what had happened to the nation during the American Revolution. If they fought the Americans again, they believed that the people would lose their homeland. It would be best for them not to take sides in the war.

All this changed when a band of Creeks known as the "Red Sticks" attacked Fort Mims in what is now Alabama. They killed nearly five hundred men, women, and children. Aroused by Tecumseh's message, the Red Sticks mounted a furious campaign to drive all the whites out of their lands. It was the beginning of the Creek War.

American forces led by General Andrew Jackson attacked the Red Sticks. Colonel Meigs, acting as the Indian agent, asked for help from the Cherokees. A group of Creek leaders also called on the Cherokees to join in the fight against the Red Sticks.

Cherokee leaders held a council meeting at Ustanali. After a lengthy debate, the council decided to aid the Americans in a campaign against the Creek rebels. John Ross drew up a declaration of war pledging the support of eight hundred warriors. Then The Ridge touched his war belt of beads. This was the ancient way to show that war had been declared. John rode to deliver the news to Jackson.

The Hermitage, as Jackson's house was called, was buzzing with activity on the morning that John arrived. John was welcomed warmly by the man whom he had met a few years earlier on his trip to the west. Jackson accepted the support of the Cherokees and chose John to be his adjutant. The Ridge was given the rank of major.

Soon the Cherokee force joined Jackson's army in the campaign against the Red Sticks. At a horseshoe-shaped bend in the Tallapoosa River, the Creek warriors had gathered to build a breastwork of logs across the open land. The only way to attack them was to cross the river or to march head-on into the barricade.

Across the Tallapoosa River the Creek canoes lay moored near the bank, moving gently with the current. On the other side six hundred Cherokees waited impatiently for battle. The crack of field artillery had died away, leaving the smell of gunpowder and a tense stillness.

John Ross waited with the others and thought about what could be done. For hours the six-pound field guns had fired against the barricade. Still, it held fast. The river could not be forded at this point, and within the barricade the Red Sticks held a hundred-acre stronghold. It was time to make a move.

John looked across at the canoes. Then, crawling back toward Jackson, he told him of his plan of action. Within minutes the Cherokees were swimming toward the Creek side of the river. Silently they took the canoes and slipped around the bend of the river in back of the barricade.

Attacking from the rear, the Cherokees made their way across the fields and charged the Red Sticks. When the Creek warriors turned to fight the Cherokees, the American soldiers attacked from the front.

As night fell, the Battle of Horseshoe Bend ended. One thousand Red Sticks died in the fierce fighting. Fifty of Jackson's forces had fallen, half of whom were Cherokees.

CHAPTER IV

Broken Promises

When the Cherokees returned to their homes, they found that American troops had stolen their horses, killed cattle and hogs, and taken corn and maple sugar. Their towns were left stripped and barren.

The Cherokees asked the U.S. government to pay for the damages. Andrew Jackson called their charges lies and used his power to delay payment to the nation. In drawing up the terms of the peace treaty with the Creeks, Jackson demanded that twenty-three million acres of land be given to the United States. Four million of those acres belonged to the Cherokees. When the Cherokees protested, they were ignored. Jackson even suggested to the War Department that it might be a good time to remove the Cherokees from their lands in Tennessee.

John Ross was surprised and shocked at the attitude of the general. The two men who had fought as allies in the Battle of Horseshoe Bend were fast becoming enemies. Ten months later, Jackson went on to become the hero of the Battle of New Orleans, which ended the War of 1812. He had become a famous and powerful man whom the Cherokees would have to reckon with in the years to come.

After the war John returned to Ross's Landing. He

After the War of 1812, Andrew Jackson became an American war hero. The Cherokees felt that he betrayed them by trying to take their land.

married Elizabeth Brown Henley, a young widow with two children whose Indian name was Quatie. Her husband had been a friend of John's, and they had known one another for most of their lives.

John built a large wooden house which was surrounded by fruit orchards and rolling pastures. In partnership with his brother Lewis, he opened a trading post that was the site of the first post office in the Cherokee Nation.

Soon John and Quatie had children of their own. They were well liked and respected among their people, and John became one of the foremost Cherokee leaders.

In February 1816, John visited President James Madison as one of six delegates from the nation. They went to Washington to clear up the mistake made by Jackson when he included Cherokee lands in the land demanded from the Creeks. John spoke for his people, too, when he asked the U.S. government to pay for the damages done by American troops during the war.

President Madison was friendly and polite. He was impressed by the way the delegates handled themselves and by the aid that the Cherokees had given to the United States. War damage claims were paid, and the Cherokee lands Jackson had asked for in his treaty were given back to the nation.

President Madison was also impressed with Andrew Jackson. While he agreed to the requests of the Cherokees, he was somewhat in awe of the Tennessee war hero. Most of what Jackson wanted, he got. Jackson was furious that the Cherokees had been given back their lands. He arranged to have himself appointed one of three U.S. commissioners to make a new land deal with the Cherokees.

The commission obtained a large tract of Cherokee land by bribing dishonest and greedy chiefs to sign a treaty. Since the chiefs who signed the treaty had no right to sell the land, the treaty was unlawful. The commissioners, however, did not let the law keep them from trying to take Cherokee lands.

Now that they had obtained a large tract of land, they decided to go a step further. They would try to persuade the Cherokees living in the East to join those in the West. Then they would be able to take all of the Cherokee land.

At this time the Cherokees who had moved west were having problems with the Osage Indians. The Osage looked at the newcomers as intruders. Because the Cherokees had no title to the western lands, the United States could not offer them protection from the Osage or from white settlers. Jackson proposed that the Cherokees agree to give up an equal amount of land in the East. Then, perhaps, an agreement could be reached. He also said that all the Cherokees might be better off in the West. By giving up their eastern lands, they could gain the "security" and "protection" of the United States.

The Cherokees who heard Jackson's words were stunned. What was this talk of establishing a nation in the West? They were a nation. They had been a nation even before the whites arrived.

The Cherokees chose a "Committee of Thirteen" to reply to the demands that they leave their lands. John Ross was chosen to head the committee. At the time John was only twenty-six years old. But he was well versed in both the English and Cherokee languages and ways of life.

John Ross and Elijah Hicks drafted a reply to Jackson.

It stated that the Cherokees chose to remain in their homeland. The Cherokees considered the matter closed. Jackson, however, did not.

Soon after Jackson received the reply to his demands, he made further offers to the Cherokees. He was not telling them to leave. That was not in his power. He was only suggesting that the Cherokees might be "happier" in the West. He offered to supply horses, goods, rifles, and help along the way if they agreed to leave their homeland.

Thirty-five hundred Cherokees, tired of the ever-present quarrel with the government, signed up to go west. These people were scorned by their fellow Cherokees for their decision to move.

In the winter of 1818, the first organized party made the journey to Arkansas. It took seventy days of travel on foot and by boat. No more than seven hundred of the thirty-five hundred who signed up actually made the long trek west to settle.

The next year, the Cherokees signed over nearly one-fourth of all the lands remaining to them to the United States. The loss of these lands left what Chief Pathkiller called "this last little." According to the treaty, "this last little" was to remain Cherokee land forever. After the twenty-five treaties the nation had signed with the whites, they hoped that this one was truly the last. Now they could look forward to a time of peace and prosperity within the nation.

Only one thing remained a threat to the Cherokees—two-thirds of Cherokee lands were claimed by the State of Georgia. The state had a little known agreement with the federal government known as the Georgia Compact of 1802.

This agreement promised to take away the Cherokees' title to their lands within the state. The Cherokees had been told nothing about the compact. When they discovered it, however, they thought that such an unfair act would be done away with or simply ignored. But the Cherokees didn't know how Governor Troup of Georgia viewed the Georgia Compact of 1802.

Governor Troup wanted the Cherokee lands turned over to the white settlers in his state. When he told the Cherokees about his plans, they listened politely and, just as politely, said they were not leaving.

When the Cherokees dismissed the demands, other means were used to try to convince them to leave. United States commissioners sought the help of William McIntosh, a Creek Indian who was the cousin of the Georgia governor. The Cherokees distrusted him because he had signed a treaty forcing his own Creek people from Georgia.

McIntosh told John Ross that the commissioners had given him twenty-one thousand dollars to offer to Cherokee officials. This payment was to be made in secret in return for an agreement that the Cherokees would go along with the commissioners' plans. John took the paper on which the sums were written. The next day, he presented the paper to the General Council meeting.

The Cherokee government was set up in the form of a legislative body. Both the National Council, or upper house, and the National Committee, or lower house, were part of the General Council. John Ross was chosen as president of the National Committee. The Ridge was elected Speaker of the House for the same body.

John rose and approached the members of the council.

Governor Troup wanted to force the Cherokees to leave their homeland so that the white settlers from Georgia could claim the land.

His recent trips to Washington on behalf of his people had left him thin and weary. Angered by McIntosh's actions, he spoke strongly about his belief in the nation.

"The author has mistaken my character and my sense of honor," he said. Then he read the offer of money to the members. The Ridge stood and spoke sharply,

"As Speaker for the Cherokee Nation, I cast McIntosh behind my back." And with those words, The Ridge turned his back on McIntosh and his offer of money. The others in the room watched as McIntosh left in disgrace.

Once more, John Ross, The Ridge, and other Cherokee leaders went to Washington. This time they spoke to President Monroe personally to ask him to do away with the Georgia Compact of 1802. In a message to Congress, the president said that the Cherokees' land was not affected by the compact. According to Monroe, the lands still belonged to the Cherokees. The United States did not have to remove the Indians as the State of Georgia wanted.

The people of Georgia felt that they had been betrayed. At this time 15,000 Cherokees lived in the nation. Georgia's population was 500,000. It is easy to see why pressure to move the Indians was so intense.

The Cherokees watched as Georgia forced the Creeks to give up all of their lands and move west. The Creeks bitterly resisted removal, but they were given no choice. Their lands and homes were taken over by anyone who wanted them.

The Cherokees vowed that this was not going to happen to them. In January they told Georgia officials that they would not give up "one foot more of land."

CHAPTER V

The Rise of the Phoenix

A paddlewheeler glided up the Savannah River on its way to Augusta where John Ross waited. On board was a twelve-hundred pound printing press for the Cherokee people. When the press was unloaded, John would see to it that it made the journey safely to New Echota by wagon.

New Echota was the new capital of the nation. Built on a level tract of land at the junction of the Coosawattee and Oostanaula rivers, it was in the very center of the Cherokee homeland. Many new buildings rose along the main street near the city square. One of these buildings would house the new printing press.

The first item to be printed on the new press would be the Cherokee alphabet. It had been invented by the silversmith, Sequoyah, one of the Cherokees who had moved to the West a few years earlier. He had made the long trip back to the East to present his gift to the nation. Sequoyah's alphabet promised to close the gap between the eastern and western Cherokees. It would unite the people once more.

John had moved his family from Ross's Landing to the head of the Coosa River in Georgia. He had built a big, two-story home surrounded by rich fields planted in cotton

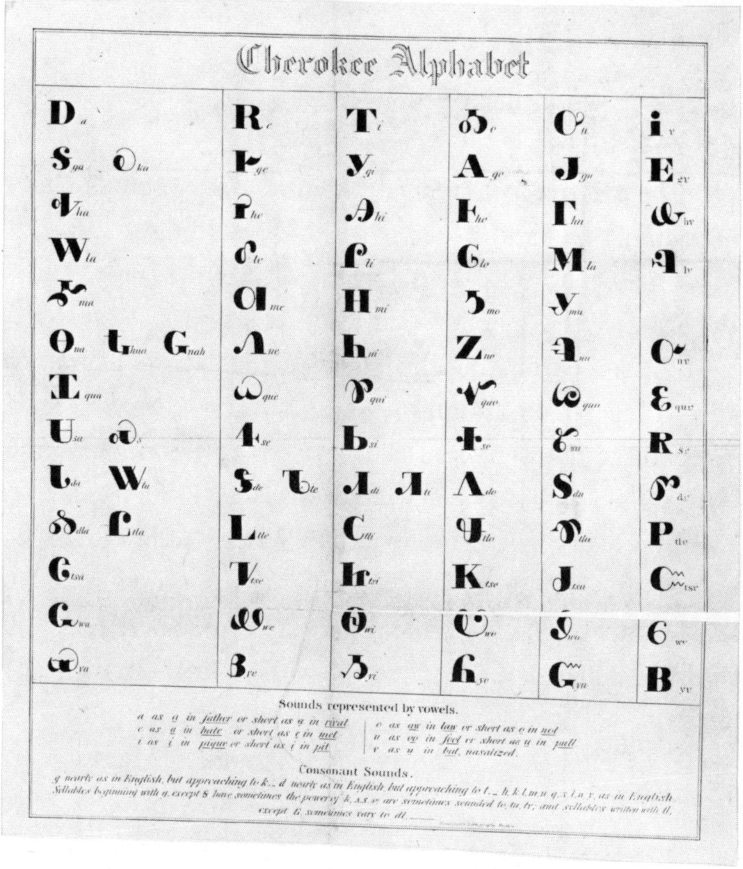

Sequoyah's alphabet meant that Cherokee children could learn to read and write in their own language.

and tobacco. The house was a rambling place filled with children and frequent guests. From his study John worked and planned for his people.

He was happy and excited about the new printing press. It would mean that all of the people would be able to read the news of their nation. Never had so much excitement been felt throughout the land. Even the youngest children had been told that they would soon learn to read and write —and in their own language!

One child who believed strongly in the nation was John Arch, or *Asti*. He walked seventy miles over the North Carolina mountains in order to learn to read and write.

When he arrived at Brainerd, the missionary school, he was filthy and tired and caked with dirt. Holding out his rifle, which was his only possession, he offered to trade it for an education. Others believed in the nation just as strongly.

At the same time that the Cherokees established a national press, they wrote a national constitution. John Ross was president of the convention that drew up the document.

It seemed that the Cherokees were becoming what John had dreamed of—an independent nation able to serve its own people. They had a constitution, a press, new businesses, and their own educational system. Soon the people would be able to read about the nation in their own newspaper.

The first edition of the paper appeared on February 21, 1828. Called the *Cherokee Phoenix,* it was printed in both the Cherokee and English languages. Elias Boudinot, the editor, wrote the first editorial. It concerned the newest move by the Georgia legislature to remove the Cherokees from their lands. Five hundred copies went out from the little print shop. The entire shop was only twenty feet by thirty feet. Most of this space was taken up by the press. It did not have a fireplace, but the enthusiasm of the *Phoenix* staff made up for any lack of heat.

Papers were sent as far away as Washington and New England and even to Europe. In the western territory, Sequoyah saw his alphabet used as a force for his people.

Later, when the press was used in the translation of the Bible, Chief Yonaguska heard the Gospel read to him for the first time. He remarked, "It seems to be a good book, but it is strange that the white people are not better, after having it for so long."

Five hundred copies of the first edition of the Cherokee Phoenix *were printed in this small print shop. The papers were sent out all over the Cherokee Nation, the United States, and even to Europe.*

Despite all the Cherokees' efforts to strengthen the nation, threatening forces were at work. Andrew Jackson was elected president of the United States. Many Americans considered Jackson a "man of the people." White people, perhaps, but not American Indians. Jackson felt that the Indians stood in the way of progress and had to be removed. One man stood squarely in his way—his former adjutant, John Ross. In the same year that Jackson was elected president, John was elected Principal Chief of the Cherokee Nation.

One month after Jackson's election, Georgia lawmakers passed an act which said that as of June 1, 1830, all Cherokee lands in the state would be subject to Georgia law. In other words, the state had declared that the Cherokees did not exist as a nation. No longer would they be free to practice their way of life.

The Cherokees drafted a protest stating that they would never surrender their rights. John Ross took the protest, which had been signed by over three thousand Cherokees, to Washington. He believed that Jackson would see him. After all, he reasoned, they had fought together, eaten together, and worked together. But Jackson refused to see John, and the protest was ignored.

Many well-known people took up the Cherokee cause. Moravians, Presbyterians, Baptists, and other church groups joined together in support of the Cherokees' right to stay in their homeland. Some of the missionaries who supported the rights of the Indians were jailed as a result of their actions.

Despite a Georgia decree that made it unlawful for Cherokees to hold meetings of their own government, John Ross called the General Council together. The council decided that any Cherokee who sold land without the nation's approval would be put to death.

The nation itself was facing death. In order to survive, the people had to use whatever weapons they had. Holding on to the land was one way.

When gold was discovered on Cherokee land in July 1829, nothing could keep the whites away. Gold seekers by the thousands poured into the area around Dahlonega in northern Georgia. It was the beginning of the gold rush in the eastern United States. The Cherokees would never recover from this blow. Greed was too strong an enemy.

Like these modern day fortune seekers, the white settlers came to Dahlonega to find gold.

One night near Dahlonega, two whites accepted the invitation of a Cherokee to share a meal at his home. Later that same night, they returned, forced the family to leave, and burned their house to the ground.

When John Ross heard what had happened, he gave orders to capture the whites and bring them to justice. Since the Cherokees were no longer allowed to govern themselves, the case was heard in a Georgia courtroom. The judge ruled that an Indian did not have the right to testify against a white person. The case was dismissed.

Acting for the Cherokee Nation, John Ross brought suit against the State of Georgia in the Supreme Court of the United States. The court ruled that the Cherokees did not have the rights of a separate nation. They had to obey the laws of the United States.

Those who supported the rights of the Cherokees were treated as outlaws. When several missionaries and the printer of the *Phoenix* refused to sign an oath of allegiance to the State of Georgia, they were arrested and put in prison. Again the case was appealed to the Supreme Court. This time the court ruled in favor of the Cherokees. Chief Justice John Marshall said that only the United States government could make laws for American Indians—the State of Georgia could not.

Georgia ignored the court ruling. And in Washington, Andrew Jackson remarked, "John Marshall has made his decision, now let him enforce it." The Cherokees did not stand a chance. Their enemies were too many and too powerful.

CHAPTER VI

"The Phantom Treaty"

It was a bitterly cold December night in 1835. The council hall was nearly empty. On the platform were The Ridge, Elias Boudinot, and U.S. government commissioners. John Ross, along with most of the Cherokee leaders, was in Washington in an effort to save the Cherokee homeland. The Ridge and Boudinot had come to believe that the only way for the Cherokees to survive as a people was to move to the West. They had called the council meeting to draw up a treaty selling Cherokee lands to the United States.

Most Cherokees stayed away from the meeting. Like John Ross, they refused to give up the Cherokee homeland. The nation had split into two opposing groups—John Ross and his followers, known as the National Party, and The Ridge, Boudinot, and their followers, known as the Treaty Party. Both sides believed they were doing what was best for the nation.

The Ridge stood up to tell why he thought the Cherokees should sign the treaty. "We obtained the land from the living God above. They [the Americans] got their title from the British. Yet they are strong and we are weak. We are few, they are many. We cannot remain here in safety and

Elias Boudinot, the editor of the Cherokee Phoenix, *was one of the leaders of the Treaty Party.*

comfort . . . . We can never forget these homes, I know, but . . . . we must leave them. I would willingly die to preserve them, but any forcible effort to keep them will cost us our lands, our lives, and the lives of our children . . . . Give up these lands and go over beyond the great Father of Waters."

After the council meeting, a committee of twenty was formed to draw up a treaty. The members agreed to sell Cherokee lands east of the Mississippi River to the United States. In return, the United States would pay the Cherokees five million dollars for their lands, the cost of removal to the West, and one year's living expenses in their new home. The treaty was signed by all members of the committee. As The Ridge put his pen to the paper, he said, "I have signed my death warrant."

According to Cherokee law, anyone who sold land without the approval of the nation would be put to death. The Ridge knew that he and the others who signed had put their lives in danger. Since the treaty had not been approved by most members of the General Council of the nation, it was not lawful. The United States, however, recognized the treaty and sent it to the Senate for final approval. It was presented to Congress as the "Treaty of New Echota." Many members of Congress knew that the treaty was unlawful and believed that it was unfair to the Cherokees. Daniel Webster called it "a great wrong."

John Ross waited in his hotel room for word on the Senate vote. In the same hotel, The Ridge waited with his party. John had been assured that the treaty would not pass. But he had also heard that Jackson had told Senate leaders that he wanted the treaty approved.

When the ballots were counted, the treaty had passed by a single vote. This vote was cast by a man who had told John Ross that he would vote against it. Hugh Lawson White changed his vote at the last minute. No one knew why.

As soon as he heard the news, John sent word to his people to ignore the treaty. He called it the "Phantom Treaty." The Cherokees were to go about their lives as usual and not worry about what might happen in the future.

When John returned home, he rode through the nation, making speeches and greeting the people. They welcomed him as a hero, even though his efforts had been in vain. When he told them to "remain united and all will be right again," he was cheered. So long as John Ross stood firm, the nation stood firm.

Jackson sent seven thousand troops to occupy Cherokee lands under the command of General John Wool. With the treaty signed, greedy men came to the nation to take their pick of houses and farms. Many Cherokees lost their homes. The land was being sold in a lottery by the State of Georgia. Even The Ridge's home had been threatened. This was not at all what he had expected when he signed the treaty. He felt that he had been betrayed.

Jackson ordered that all arms and weapons be taken away from the Cherokees. Soon General Wool discovered that the people had very few arms. They owned some shotguns and hunting rifles, but most of the people had no knowledge of firearms. The closest they came to fighting was with a few squirrels or some deer.

Within a few short weeks, General Wool began to find his job a "heart-rending one." He had come prepared to

General Wool was not prepared for what he found in the Cherokee lands.

find a cruel, warlike people. Jackson, however, had not prepared him for the truth. Wool wrote to Secretary of War Cass that if he could, he would remove every single Cherokee—not to please Jackson or the State of Georgia—but to protect them from the unruly whites who seized their homes and farms.

General Wool sent a message to Jackson from John Ross. "Not only do I consider the treaty a corrupt fraud," said John. "But I declare it null and void." Jackson was furious that Wool had sent him a message from John Ross. He told the general that as far as he was concerned, the Cherokee Nation did not exist.

John continued to travel through the nation to tell the people to ignore the Treaty of New Echota. The State of Georgia considered him to be a dangerous man and had him closely watched by state guardsmen. This, however, did not stop John. He stepped up his efforts to unite the Cherokees against the plan to force them from their homeland.

In the spring John returned to his home after many weeks of traveling. When he opened the door, he found a strange man standing in his hallway with a rifle in his hands. The man told John that he had won the Ross property in the Georgia lottery and had come to claim it. Quatie and the children were inside. He had allowed them to stay until John's return.

Overnight, John had lost his fine home, his cattle, his fields, and his business. The ferry had been taken over by other strangers. These gaunt-faced men with guns were the "new settlers" who claimed Cherokee lands as their own.

CHAPTER VII

The Trail of Tears

Snow lay in soft curves on the hills. Children played in the cold, crisp air where the breath of horses made frosty clouds. In the early twilight blue shadows lengthened and faded into darkness. Other shadows spread over the land—shadows that lay heavy over the peaceful towns of the Cherokees.

In that January of 1837, six hundred Cherokees prepared to leave the nation. No U.S. troops were there to make them go. These wealthy families had chosen to leave their lands while they could still travel on their own. They had been paid for their homes and farms, and they took their personal belongings with them. These Treaty Party followers were known as the Ridge Party. To John Ross they were traitors.

With a group of Cherokee leaders, John went once more to Washington to try to reason with the U.S. government. Standing in the bright sunlight on Pennsylvania Avenue, he watched the crowds cheer and the bands play as Andrew Jackson passed by in his carriage. Jackson and Martin Van Buren were on their way to the place where Van Buren would be sworn in as the president of the United States. John hoped that unlike Jackson, the new president would respect the rights of the Cherokees.

John Ross went to Washington, D.C., many times to try to save the land of his people.

A few days later, John was granted an interview with Van Buren. The president listened to him politely. Later, however, the Cherokees were informed that Van Buren would continue Jackson's removal plans. All American Indians in the East would be forced to move west of the Mississippi River. John returned to the nation, defeated.

While John had been in Washington trying to preserve the nation, the U.S. Army had been busy destroying it. Armed troops had begun to build stockades to hold the Cherokees prisoner until they started the long journey west. Now the once peaceful towns looked more like armed camps.

General R. G. Dunlap was in charge of building the stockades. He had watched as, day by day, the Cherokees lost their homes and belongings, but never their dignity. When the stockades were completed, he told his troops that he would do no more. He had carried out his orders to build the stockades, but he would not fill them with Cherokees. Someone else would have to fill the prison camps.

President Van Buren chose General Winfield Scott to carry out the final steps for removal. Orders came from Washington to put the Cherokees in the stockades. Sometimes the Cherokees were hardly out of their homes before the whites moved in. Troops had to escort Indian families to prevent them from being injured by unruly groups of settlers.

At New Echota General Scott took over the council house as his headquarters. Scott warned the troops under his command not to mistreat the Cherokees. Roaming bands of whites, however, took advantage of the confusion to sack Cherokee towns and rob the people. Sometimes the troops, too, did not follow the general's orders. One such case involved a Cherokee named Tsali.

Tsali, his wife, sons, and brother were led at bayonet point from their village toward the stockade on the Hiwassee River. During the march a soldier whipped Tsali's wife with a gun butt when she stopped to care for the needs of her baby. Tsali tried to protect his wife, and in the fight that followed a soldier was killed. Tsali and his family fled to a secret cave in the Great Smoky Mountains. Other Cherokees heard about Tsali, and they, too, fled to the mountains.

When General Scott heard what had happened, he said that Tsali and his family must be captured. He believed that if one small group of Cherokees escaped, soon others would follow. The general sent for William Thomas, a trader who had lived for twenty years in the nation and was trusted by the Cherokees. Thomas was given a message to take to Tsali. If Tsali would surrender with his family, the message said, a deal could be made. The Cherokees who had fled to the mountains with Tsali would be allowed to remain in the East. He and his family, however, would be tried and punished by the U.S. Army.

Tsali agreed to the general's offer and returned with his family to surrender. At dawn the next morning, Tsali, his brother, and all but one of his sons were executed by a firing squad. His youngest son was spared because of his youth. Because of Tsali's act of courage, the Cherokees who escaped removal kept the nation alive in the East. Today their descendants still live in the Great Smoky Mountains.

How must they have felt, these Cherokees, as they were forced from their lands? Behind them were the gentle, rolling hills, the herb gardens and the apple orchards, the well-fed cattle and the carefully tended fields which they had plowed and planted and cared for. Their lands were as much a part of them as their bodies and they were torn away, removed from the earth which had given life to them and their ancestors.

John Ross needed time to think, to be alone. He knew of the times when his ancestors had spoken to the spirit of the grandfathers through the rising smoke of the pipe. Looking toward his beloved mountains, he called on the spirit of the old ones. John believed strongly in his faith and in his people. Even though his world was crumbling, he had to remain strong in order to help the Cherokees. He asked for strength to lead them in the journey ahead and to help them rebuild their lives.

If the people had to leave their homeland, John wanted them to do it on their own, with honor, as a nation. He toured the stockades and came up with a plan in which the Cherokees would carry out their own removal. If they had to go, they would organize their own parties and make their own travel plans. John formed thirteen parties of Cherokees, about one thousand in each group, to make the long journey.

The summer of 1838 was very hot and dry. For months the rains did not come. Within the walls of the stockades, the Cherokees suffered greatly. The people had always lived as free as the great hawks that soared over the valley. Now they were captured and held as prisoners inside the airless, cramped quarters of the camps. Many of them grew sick and died.

In spite of the heat and drought, the U.S. Army forced some Cherokees to start on the trip west in June. The people had little water to drink, and what food they had spoiled

In what became known as the Trail of Tears, the Cherokees were forced to leave their homeland and move west of the Mississippi River.

quickly in the heat. Traveling by open flatboats and overcrowded railroad cars made it difficult to rest or sleep. In these conditions, many of the children, old people, and newborn babies died along the way.

John Ross persuaded General Scott to postpone the removal of the rest of the people until the fall when the weather would be cooler. Using Cherokee national funds, John tried to provide the people with food and clothing for the long trip ahead of them. The Cherokees received little help from the U.S. government. A small amount of supplies was given to each person before they left.

On October 1 the first group of Cherokees organized by John Ross left for the West. Traveling in wagons, on horses, and on foot, they followed an overland route—northwest through Tennessee and Kentucky, across the southern tip of Illinois, and southwestward through what is now Missouri and Arkansas to the Indian Territory. Early in November the last wagon train left the Cherokee homeland. John was with them.

The fall rains, the winter cold, and the constant travel took their toll on the Cherokees. Winter came early that year, and when the people reached the Mississippi, the river was frozen. The ice was too thin to support the weight of the wagons, but too thick to allow boats to cross. The Cherokees waited and died.

As many as 20 people were buried by the side of the trail every day. A traveler who came across one of the wagon trains wrote that he saw old women stumbling barefoot on the frozen mud. Of the 17,000 people who began the journey, more than 1,500 died along the way. In the stockades 2,500 more had died. Nearly one-fourth of the Cherokee

Nation was killed by the Indian removal carried out by the United States government.

Much has been written about what the Cherokees call the Trail of Tears. This letter from an old soldier to his grandchildren tells what it was like to be there.

"Children:

"This is my birthday, December 11, 1890. I am eighty years old today. . . .

"The removal of the Cherokee Indians from their lifelong homes in the year 1838 found me a young man in the prime of life and a Private soldier in the American Army. I saw helpless Cherokees arrested and dragged from their homes, and driven at bayonet point into the stockades. And in the chill of a drizzling rain on an October morning I saw them loaded like cattle or sheep into 645 wagons and started toward the west.

"One can never forget the sadness and solemnity of that morning. Chief John Ross led in prayer and when the bugle sounded and the wagons started rolling, many of the children rose to their feet and waved their hands goodby to their mountain homes, knowing they were leaving them forever. Many of these helpless people did not have blankets and many of them had been driven from home barefooted.

"On the morning of November 17, we encountered a terrific sleet and snow storm with freezing temperatures and from that day until we reached the end of the fateful journey . . . the sufferings of the Cherokees were awful. The trail of the exiles was a trail of death. They had to sleep in the wagons and on the ground without fire. And I have known as many as twenty-two of them die in one night of pneumonia due to ill treatment, cold and exposure.

"Murder is murder whether committed by the villain skulking in the dark or by uniformed men stepping to the strains of martial music. Murder is murder and somebody must answer, somebody must explain the streams of blood that flowed in the Indian country in the summer of 1838 . . . I wish I could forget it all, but the picture of 645 wagons lumbering over the frozen ground with their Cargo of suffering humanity still lingers in my memory . . . .

"Children—Thus ends my promised birthday story. This December the 11th, 1890."

On the trail, John had watched Quatie grow pale and silent. She fell ill with pneumonia after she gave her blanket to a sick child to keep warm. The child recovered, but Quatie did not. She died on the riverboat *Victoria* at Little Rock, Arkansas, on February 1, 1839. John left the boat to bury her in the frozen ground. There he had to leave her.

Many others were left—small children, old people, young men and women, parents, sisters, and brothers. They all lie along the trail.

Another soldier who witnessed the sad event said later, "I fought through the Civil War and have seen men shot to pieces and slaughtered by the thousands, but the Cherokee Removal was the cruelest work I ever knew."

CHAPTER VIII

A Nation Divided

The trail ended for John's group at Fort Gibson in what is now Oklahoma. Then it was called "Indian Territory." John and his party were the last to arrive, and they were welcomed by the earlier settlers. For the families who were brought together again, it was a happy time. But for the many who had lost friends and loved ones on the long trail west, it was a time for sadness.

A General Council was called to bring the early and late settlers together. It was time to rebuild their lives and their nation. Although they had been through too much to allow politics to divide them now, the meeting was torn with arguments.

The "Late Emigrants," as John Ross's followers were called, had been welcomed warmly, and yet they were viewed with some suspicion. The early settlers were the wealthier Cherokees who had built nice homes and established a community. Since many of them belonged to the Treaty Party that had backed the sale of Cherokee lands, they saw John Ross and his followers as a threat to their government. They told the Late Emigrants that although they would be allowed to vote and run for public office, they would be subject to the laws that were already made.

The Cherokees called a General Council to try to rebuild their nation in the new land. (Courtesy Oklahoma Historical Society)

John Ross took the stand they had feared. He called for a "new government West of the River Mississippi." He wanted all the Cherokees to vote to decide how they would be governed. The early settlers replied that the government was working well and needed no changes. With each meeting bad feeling grew on both sides.

Many of the late settlers blamed the Treaty Party for much of the suffering they had endured. If the Treaty Party had not sold out, they said, the rest of the Cherokees would have had a better chance to fight removal. Some of them vowed to seek revenge when they reached the West.

A few days later The Ridge, his son John, and Elias Boudinot were murdered by unknown assassins. Only Stand Watie, the brother of Elias Boudinot, escaped the attack. Watie, who was a powerful member of the Treaty Party, accused John Ross of being responsible for the murders.

When John heard about the killings, he was warned that he would pay for them with his life. At once he asked the commanding general at Fort Gibson to find out who had killed the men. John was innocent, and he wanted his name cleared of the charges.

General Arbuckle was convinced that John had either ordered the murders or was hiding the killers. He asked John to visit him at the fort to discuss the matter. But after talking with his friends, John decided he had acted unwisely in asking for help from the army. He did not go to see the general. He believed that the killings were a Cherokee matter and should be handled by Cherokees.

The murders made the divisions in the nation worse than ever, but John called for everyone to keep the peace. Three months later, he was elected Principal Chief of the Cherokee

Nation in the West. On September 6, 1839, a new constitution was written at Tahlequah, which had been chosen as the national capital.

For several years the new nation suffered from crime, violence, and drunkenness. The Trail of Tears had left deep scars that required time to heal. In time, however, the different parties began working for the common good of the Cherokee people.

John Ross was one of those who was able to take root in the new land. He married a young Quaker woman from Philadelphia named Mary Stapler. They built a home which they called Rose Cottage after the roses that climbed over the doorways and bloomed in the gardens of its broad lawns. A thousand acres surrounded the house. Near it were well-stocked smoke houses, granaries, a dairy, and a large stable which quartered fine horses and an elegant carriage.

In 1846 John made a trip to Washington to meet with President James Polk. After a great deal of talk, a treaty was signed in which the claims of the new emigrants and the old settlers were resolved. A general pardon was granted for all past offenses within the nation. John Ross and Stand Watie shook hands at last, and with that simple action, the Cherokee Nation was reunited.

The next few years were good ones for the Cherokees in the West. Eleven public schools were opened together with four mission schools. Now the Cherokee children could attend schools from kindergarten through high school.

There were many new houses and farms in the nation. People raised healthy cattle and horses, and fields rich with corn and wheat lay over the land. It seemed that the nation would grow and prosper.

John and Mary built a beautiful new home which they called Rose Cottage. Their home was one of the finest in the new land.

Then, rumors of war were heard. At Tahlequah, John watched sadly as his people took opposing sides in the War Between the States. The Cherokee Nation was divided into two groups: the Treaty Party, led by Stand Watie, sided with the South. Most of the early settlers joined this group. They were members of a society called the Knights of the Golden Circle.

The other group was the National Party, which supported the Union cause. They, too, formed a society called "Pin." Its members wore crossed pins on their shirts.

As the Confederate Army marched along the Cherokee border toward Arkansas, feeling ran high among the Indians. Ross called a meeting of the National Council. Four thousand Cherokees came to decide what the nation should do. Would they declare for the South or the North?

Some of the people were so young that they remembered little about life in the Cherokee homeland. The mountains and valleys of Georgia, Tennessee, and North Carolina were places they had only heard about, but never seen. Yes, they had heard the stories from their fathers and grandfathers of the soft and gentle lands. And in some, memories of those lands stirred.

The Cherokees declared their support for the South. And once more, John Ross and Stand Watie stood together. They shook hands in friendship and John said, "In time of war, we must fight together. As Brothers live, as Brothers die!"

Stand Watie became a general in the Confederate Army. Soon war became a way of life as the Indian Territory was turned into a battlefield. Much of the nation was left as charred ruins and scorched fields. When Union forces in-

Like Stand Watie, many Cherokees fought in the Civil War for the Confederate Army. Others took the Union side. (Courtesy Oklahoma Historical Society)

vaded Cherokee lands, John was taken prisoner and Rose Cottage was burned to the ground.

John was taken to Philadelphia where he was treated as a prisoner on parole. Later, when he was allowed to travel, John met with President Lincoln in Washington. He spoke with the president about the needs of the Cherokee Nation.

Lincoln offered friendship to John Ross and to the Cherokees despite the fact that they had supported the South. Lincoln wanted to see his country healed of the wounds of war.

If Lincoln had not been murdered, the Cherokees might have fared better. But the next president shared neither Lincoln's views nor his compassion. After the war, the United States declared that because the Cherokees had supported the South, they had given up any rights made under the treaty at the time of removal. The government stopped all payments to the Indians and opened up their lands to outsiders. The Cherokee Nation was broken.

John Ross was in ill health. His wife Mary had died, and he was growing weaker. Now, at seventy-six years of age, he had been Principal Chief of the Cherokees for forty years. In Philadelphia he was separated from his people, and they needed him.

Shortly after the end of the war, a meeting was held at Fort Smith, Arkansas. Indian leaders and U.S. government officials came to work out a new treaty.

John's people waited for him anxiously. They wondered if he would be able to make the long journey to Arkansas. John did not let down his people. When he arrived, the meetings had already begun. The Cherokees welcomed him warmly. But the United States commissioners were not so happy to see him.

Commissioner Dennis Cooley spoke harshly:

"We believe John Ross to be still an enemy of the United States." He said that the government no longer recognized Ross as Principal Chief of the Cherokees.

John requested permission to speak.

"I had three sons in your army," he said, "and three grandsons and three nephews. I came here with the hope that I might be useful to my people, not for the purpose of resisting the policies of the United States."

Before the meeting ended, John had gathered support from the government for his own party. But the meeting and the long journey proved too much for the aging leader. He collapsed and was taken to the home of a relative.

A month later, the Cherokees called a National Council meeting. Once more, as they had so many times in the past, they pledged their loyalty to John Ross. Soon after, in August 1865, John died.

At his last public appearance John Ross remarked, "I am still John Ross, the same John Ross of former years. Unchanged! No cause for change!"

And he didn't change—through removal, in exile, in peace, and in war. He served his people for over half a century.

John Ross sleeps with his people.

THE AUTHOR

Raised in Savannah, Georgia, Sara Gordon Harrell has been interested in the history and culture of the American Indian for many years. In a previous book written for the "Story of an American Indian" series, *Tomo-chi-chi,* she wrote about a Creek leader who lived in the area where she spent her childhood. Her interest in the history of the South and the American Indians who once shared its land led to writing a biography of John Ross.

As a free-lance writer, Ms. Harrell has written numerous nature and science articles for magazines and newspapers, including the *Atlanta Constitution. John Ross: The Story of an American Indian* is her third book for children. She attended Georgia Southern College, the University of North Carolina at Chapel Hill, and Emory University. Ms. Harrell lives in Kenner, Louisiana, with her husband and son.

Photographs reproduced through the courtesy of the American Museum of Natural History, the Tourist Division of the Georgia Bureau of Industry and Trade, the Tourist Division, Georgia Department of Community Development, the Georgia Department of Archives and History, the Georgia Historical Commission, the Library of Congress, the Oklahoma Historical Society, the Smithsonian Institution, Anthropological Archives, the Western History Collection of the University of Oklahoma Library, and the Woolaroc Museum.

OTHER BIOGRAPHIES
IN THIS SERIES ARE

William Beltz
Robert Bennett
Black Hawk
Joseph Brant
Crazy Horse
Geronimo
Oscar Howe
Pauline Johnson
Chief Joseph
Maria Martinez
George Morrison
Daisy Hooee Nampeyo
Michael Naranjo
Osceola
Powhatan
Red Cloud
Sacagawea
Sealth
Sequoyah
Sitting Bull
Maria Tallchief
Tecumseh
Jim Thorpe
Tomo-chi-chi
Pablita Velarde
William Warren
Annie Wauneka